BLUFF YOUR WAY IN
IN
LAW

MARTIN VERNON

RAVETTE PUBLISHING

Published by Ravette Publishing Limited
P.O. Box 296
Horsham
West Sussex RH13 8FH

Telephone: (01403) 711443
Fax: (01403) 711554

First printed 1995
Reprinted 1996
Updated 1997

Series Editor – Anne Tauté

Cover design – Jim Wire, Quantum
Printing & binding – Cox & Wyman Ltd.
Production – Oval Projects Ltd.

The Bluffer's Guides series is based
on an original idea by Peter Wolfe.

The Bluffer's Guides™, Bluffer's™
and Bluff Your Way™ are Trademarks.

An Oval Project
for Ravette Publishing.

CONTENTS

INTRODUCTION

The law is a giant subject. It covers everything that everyone does or does not do and why they should or should not do it.

The main problem is that it consists only of words. Medicine is different: cutting, stitching, drugging, transplanting; action is mixed with the mystique. Accountancy has calculating, percentaging, proportionalising, projecting; its meaning delightfully obscured by sheets of figures. Philosophy has its wondrous obfuscations and obscurities; archaeology has its hidden mysteries; the sciences have their arcane complexities and music its tonal subtleties. Not so the law.

Anyone can read the words of law, anyone can express an instant opinion, anyone can offer criticism, anyone can (and will) tell of a relevant experience. In short, it is difficult for the bluffer to be different. Jargon is not enough. In law you must go further and pretend a depth of knowledge and a breadth of understanding that will rise above the superficial comment of the barrack room lawyer and confound the instant soundbite of the pseudo expert.

But beware. The law is a profession where to pretend a qualification or personate a lawyer may be an offence – a sure way of obtaining a closer acquaintance with the law than was intended.

It is to your advantage that few members of the public understand the structure of the law and most lawyers prefer not to know too much about the law itself. Keeping up to date with a zillion new cases every day is tiring. What is of importance to the lawyer, and thence to the bluffer, is to know something about the different branches of the law together with just enough snippets of fact to get by in at least some of them.

Those who seek to explore the delectable realms of equity and succession, of jurisprudence or revenue law, of licensing or mercantile law, of banking or the law of construction must pursue their quest in heavier tomes than this slim publication. It is enough to keep in mind that you only need the necessary framework and enough inside information to impress and, who knows, if you display sufficient stubborn determination and a consuming desire to put cost before justice you may yet achieve the ultimate goal of the bluffer – the post of Lord Chancellor.

THE ENGLISH LEGAL SYSTEM

The English legal system* is adversarial as opposed to inquisitorial. What this means is that lawyer A tries to outwit lawyer B and the court decides on the winner by adding up points for technical merit and artistic impression. Inquisitorial systems expect the judge to find out much more for himself which is not half as confrontational and therefore much less fun.

To bluff well in the law, you need to know something about how laws are made. Some of it you can blame on lawyers because judges made the law and all judges were lawyers once (just as most gamekeepers used to do a bit of poaching). The 'Common Law' is the name for the bits which originated in common custom and were then developed by the decisions of the judges (and you might be right in thinking that it is an odd name for something developed by people who went to schools like Eton or Charterhouse).

It used to be true that the rest of the law was made by Parliament, but that was before the European Union came along. Most European Law is designed by French bureaucrats of little brain as revenge for Agincourt and is voted through by failed former local government politicians from various countries. English Statute law has been created by well meaning (if small minded) British politicians who thought they had some sort of mandate at the time.

Leaving European Law on one side (and there are more imaginative places to put it) a useful distinction by sheer volume of the English legal system is to visualise the two great reference works of the law,

* Which embraces the English and the Welsh, but is ignored by the Scots who have their own version.

Halsbury's Laws and *Halsbury's Statutes*. Each sports fifty to sixty volumes plus noters-up, and annual updates; but all one needs to know is that just about everything is in one or the other. If it is not in the *Statutes* then it was not made by Parliament, which means it must be in the *Laws* and so part of the Common Law. Simple really (except that it will cost you a year's salary to buy the books).

You are encouraged to conveniently and carelessly ignore the vast panoply of constitutional and administrative law. This mind-blowingly exciting subject embraces the functions of Parliament, the Church, the State, the Judiciary and those amazing convolutions of what are quaintly called the 'organs of government'.

Putting aside strong temptation to call for a transplant of the latter, you will find that all these wonders combine to direct the constitutional position of the Subject and his rights and duties. Better still, such diversions as the Royal Prerogative and Doctrine of State Necessity jostle for attention. Whether nowadays the parallel issues of what is called 'the Separation of Powers', likewise 'the Royal Pleasure', have anything to do with the alleged infidelities of sundry members of the Royal Family is not for us to speculate.

Just as the apes evolved into man, so constitutional conventions evolved into the Rule of Law. Not for the English and Welsh the rigid formality of faddish Bills of Rights beloved of American and Continental administrations, but something of individuality and flexibility on which one can hold forth, safe in the knowledge that none will contradict, since attempts to study the subject drive most lawyers into a deep sleep.

Stick to the premise that most criminal law and an awful lot of civil law is made by Parliament. There have been good Parliaments and bad Parliaments and hence there are good laws and bad laws depending on whom you voted for at the time. What one party sees as a nifty bit of legislation to squeeze the rich and give to the poor, the opposition will see as the betrayal of life itself. This used to mean that when the opposition got into power they stuck their own politically correct Lord Chancellor on the Woolsack (an enormous red mattress clearly designed for orgies) and he changed the laws round again. Such changes were usually in the areas of the three 'R's' – Rented property, Redundancy and Rape. These days Chancellors are more concerned with the three S's – Saving money, Speeding up the law, and Spoiling it for Solicitors.

Bluffers will find the newest laws give them greatest scope because of the present devious scheme of hiding away in each new Statute a clause saying that it does not actually come into effect until another paper is published at some future indeterminate date. This is wonderful fun, not only because lawyers do not know whether the Statute applies or not, but also because they buy the volume containing the Statute many years before they need it, thus ruining their profitability. They then have to buy an entirely separate book called *What's in Force?* to help them along. It is this delicious uncertainty that can be exploited with impunity.

The Law of Precedent

The law of precedent is created by one court reckoning it is brighter than another court and setting a precedent that the lower court has to follow. This is a marvellous opportunity for judges who have got a bit above themselves to slap the wrists of the lower court judge who probably knocked them for six in some case in the Nuneaton County Court years ago. You only need to know the names of a few famous judges and to invent the names of a few cases. It is good strategy when talking of judges to use the expression "as he then was" to show that you know the judge in question was promoted to some more exotic fat cat job later.

In the law, Latin looms large as a necessary weapon in the armoury, and the distinction between *'ratio decidendi'* and *'obiter dictum'* is a useful one to know. Where a judgment is being given, the *'ratio decidendi'* is the precise bit that is actually relevant to the case in point and intended to hit the button as the precedent for the future. The *'obiter dictum'* means the judge in question was banging on about something else at the time so one need not take much notice of what he said.

There being billions of reported cases, and few lawyers knowing the names of more than a handful of them, brazenly bold bluffers can often get away with throw-away comments such as: "Was it not Mr. Justice Wilberforce (as he then was) who said something to that effect, 'obiter' of course, in the case of Higginbotham against Woolworths reported at 1947 CA 1297?" (CA is short for Court of Appeal and there are similar codes for other courts and tribunals, easy familiarity with which should ensure your verisimilitude.)

Civil Law or Criminal Law

The law is decided on the basis of wrongs and rights. A wrong is a breach of a rule and can be moral, in which case have a word with the Campaign for Moral Rights brigade, but do not waste your money on lawyers; or it can be legal, in which case it can be civil or criminal, or occasionally both if you really try hard.

Civil law is all about people's rights and duties to one another and covers dozens of different and complex subjects, all enormous on their own and all subdivided into dozens more areas which are just as complicated. Each of those areas will have its textbooks and specialists. This allows you to pretend a rare speciality (such as 'employment contracts of second division football managers' or 'environmental law and the wood louse') and then to feign ignorance of any law outside that field.

There are some exceptionally trying bits of civil law like property and succession (the latter being all about what happens to your things when you fall off your perch) which have nothing to do with wrongs, but as a rule in civil law you just look around for someone to sue and off you go. That makes you the Plaintiff, the person you are suing the Defendant, and at least two lawyers very happy.

Criminal law is all about the duties you owe to society, which means the state, and is generally not only easier but much more exciting than civil law. It mainly consists of sex and violence with a bit of car chasing thrown in. Arguing the criminal degree of sexual penetration required to constitute bestiality with a sheep is much more stimulating than disputing the civil rights in respect of your client's neighbour's fence.

Criminal lawyers are both actors and posers – full of dramatic gestures, headline grabbing soundbites, pregnant pauses and cutting questions. The latter are designed either to intimidate or to throw dust in the eyes of the average juror (though the 'average' juror bears little relation to anyone you may regard as average in normal life).

11

The Courts

The distinction between criminal law and civil law is one that needs to be kept in mind.

Criminal Cases

These start in the Magistrates Court, go from there to the Crown Court, go to appeal to the Court of Appeal (Criminal Division) and then have it all set aside by being the subject of a programme on television.

In the provinces there will be magistrates courts in sundry places in most towns. Some are attached to police stations, some are in old town halls, some in tasteless sixties concrete slabs, and some in modern red brick and glass emporia. Some even serve a dual purpose: the one in Ashbourne in Derbyshire used to double up as an indoor market and the court was conducted from trestle tables rearranged for the purpose.

In London you will find that magistrates courts are dotted around in odd places. Some are jolly convenient: appear at Great Marlborough Street and you can shop at Liberty's while you're waiting for your case to come on (probably called Liberty's because they let you off so you can shop afterwards).

Crown courts vary from towering dark panelled Victorian structures where judges can look down on their prey from a commanding height, to modernistic mullioned stone and shimmering glass palaces which each cost about as much as the annual expenditure on the legal aid fund. They are often sub-divided into suites: the barristers' suite, the solicitors' suite, the judges' suite, the custodial suite.

The London Crown court is the famous Old Bailey. Real lawyers call it 'the Bailey' for short.

Civil Cases

Smaller civil cases start in the County Court. When the County Court gets it wrong, you appeal to the High Court. When they foul up, you present it in the Court of Appeal. The really brave (and rich) losers have a bash in the House of Lords.

Bigger (or sometimes more peculiar) civil cases start in the High Court which, like the football league, is divided into divisions. The main division is called the **Queen's Bench** (think of a long back-less throne), then there is the **Family Division**, which is an odd name since any family is well and truly broken up before a relevant case gets there. The best is the **Chancery Division** because no-one is ever quite sure what it does save that cases last eight times as long and are deeply dull. It is possible to identify Chancery Division barristers by the cloud of dust that hovers around them.

The main High Court building in London is the extravagant and extraordinary Gothic pile dominating the Strand whose archway entrance features on the news with monotonous regularity. This whole complex is called the Royal Courts of Justice. There is a wondrous vaulted marble hall surrounded by the evocative old courts of the Master of the Rolls, the Lord Chief Justice, the Chancellor of England (who sadly has nothing to do with the Exchequer) and other lesser lights.

The Royal Courts of Justice contain the Bear Garden which is neither for teddy bears nor polar bears but is the waiting area for lots of chambers. Chambers are not old fashioned privies but court rooms in which Masters make orders. Masters can be women but they must not be called Mistresses.

Lurking around chambers will be found 'Outdoor Clerks' despite the fact that they spend all their time

13

indoors talking on mobile telephones.

There are also whole hosts of other courts: Mercantile and Commercial Courts, the Patent Court, Industrial and all sorts of other Tribunals; even the Official Referees have a slinky building on Fetter Lane all to themselves (but then referees always did have to have separate changing rooms).

Amateurs will be happiest in County Courts, where Do-it-Yourself law is encouraged (DIYers are called 'litigants in person') so everyone can and does join in. If you have not yet had a go, beat a path to your nearest county court, it has probably been rebuilt alongside the Crown Court in recent years, and go for it – issue your own summons. Here also is likely to be the High Court office (or Registry) for issuing writs – even more fun for the dedicated who want to gain first hand experience.

The only snag is that the fees paid to the government for issuing proceedings are doubling and tripling by the year. It is all part of 'making law pay', (quite why law should have to pay for itself is obscure – the army and the police force do not have to). Still, to balance the ever increasing court fees collected by the state, the costs actually allowed to lawyers through the court system are made smaller so it's not all bad.

The best route for bluffers is to mention the European Court of Justice. Going to the European Court will probably prolong a decision for at least a couple of decades and produce a completely different result. This is because their Judges come from countries that have Bills of Rights or written constitutions. Since the English do not have any truck with such new fangled ideas, and as there are more French, German, Dutch, etc. judges than English ones in the European Court, they are always right and the English are always wrong.

Alternatively, you could start a discussion about the law in Scotland. Scottish Civil law is governed by the Court of Session which is divided into an Outer House and an Inner House. The latter has first and second divisions so that Rangers and Celtic supporters can feel involved. Appeal to the Inner House and you will find yourself travelling south to the House of Lords or across the Channel to the random vagaries of the European Court of Justice.

Point out that instead of County Courts the Scots have sheriffdoms, and that Plaintiffs and Defendants are unknown in Scotland, they are replaced by Pursuers and Defenders who have strange arsenals of tactics such as arrestments and inhibitions. Inhibitions can be recalled (perhaps under deep hypnosis). Damages can be replaced by 'Reparations', tort is unknown – what a fearful place for an English civil lawyer.

Barristers in Scotland are called advocates, but the posers amongst them can still aspire to be Queen's Counsel. Posing extends to some solicitors also since a group of them, mainly based in Edinburgh, use the initials W.S., to denote that they are members of the Society of Writers to Her Majesty's Signet – it is thought that the expression has something of a ring to it. An even smaller body of Scottish solicitors are S.S.C.'s, denoting membership of the Society of Solicitors to the Supreme Courts of Scotland. In fact, all English solicitors are 'Solicitors of the Supreme Court' but they don't feel such a need to have letters after their names.

Their criminal court is oddly known as the High Court of Justiciary which has its Lords Commissioners who control the Lords Advocate's department wherein beings such as 'advocates depute' and 'procurators fiscal' move in their mysterious ways.

One of the other novel things about Scottish criminal

procedure is that most High Court trials have fifteen jurors instead of the usual dozen. However there is less chance of a failure to agree since a majority of only eight to seven will carry the day.

Remind others, too, that Scottish criminal law has an alternative verdict to guilty and not guilty, the famous not proven verdict which neatly leaves it open as to whether you are or aren't.

The Lawyers

The name 'lawyer' covers solicitors, barristers, legal executives, academics and sundry others. The confident would-be legal beagle might talk of 'we lawyers' with less risk of contradiction or prosecution than might be encountered by plumping for a specific qualification.

Lawyers can be broken down (indeed, many of them are) as follows:

Solicitors

Solicitors are the salt of the earth. Caring, considerate, and kind. Intellectually brilliant but down to earth and approachable. Superb lawyers, witty, charming, sensual and attractive. Skilled at management, marketing, information technology, and staff relations. Hardworking, sober and always well dressed. Completely unbiased.

This is a typical thumbnail sketch. If you find a solicitor who fails to meet these criteria, contact the Office for the Supervision of Solicitors at Redditch. Everyone else does.

Barristers

Barristers are referred to by solicitors as 'counsel'. This serves to confuse both the client and the average typist. The solicitor will dictate something like: 'Counsel advised that the Council should, as a counsel of perfection, instruct their Counsel to respond'. This will appear in print: 'Counsel advises that the counsel should as a council of perfection, instruct the council to respond' and with luck the client will be too fearful to ask for an explanation.

Barristers think they are cleverer than solicitors, which is odd because the bar exams taken by barristers used to be easier than the exams taken by solicitors, but then barristers also have to eat dinners in order to qualify and perhaps this provides intellectual food to make up the difference. It does not matter of course, because the rest of the population is convinced that a barrister is something a solicitor becomes if he is exceedingly clever, and is incapable of being convinced to the contrary. All solicitors become used to smiling sweetly when asked if they hope to qualify as a barrister one day.

In court barristers call each other 'my learned friend' just before they insult each other. Solicitors are only allowed to be called 'my friend', and very learned-looking solicitors who get mistaken for barristers have to tell the court they are not 'learned' at all.

Barristers never shake hands with each other; they say this is because there are so few of them they should all know each other. This allows you the fun of introducing unknown barristers to each other and watching them get all embarrassed when they have shaken hands by mistake.

Barristers are like badgers. This is because they live

individual lives in worlds of their own called setts. In fact it is spelled 'sets' and consists of chambers. These sets of chambers are run on committee lines with an elected 'head of chambers' but dominated by a clerk (*q.v.*) who runs the administrative and financial life of each individual. Barristers also have to join an Inn. Some of these are called temples which is probably why some barristers expect you to worship the ground they walk on.

Young barristers can be easy meat and a reasonable solicitor may neatly dismantle them in court. But beware. Young barristers become older barristers very quickly and then have an unhappy habit of becoming judges. Judges are like elephants, they never forget.

There are masses of women barristers. They are all either young and incredibly beautiful, or old and incredibly stubborn. They can be very unpredictable when they haven't got any briefs. Briefs are important to barristers. So are wigs. A young woman barrister in a wig can produce an effect similar to wearing fishnet stockings and suspenders.

Barristers also have bags. The younger ones have blue bags and the older ones have reddy-mauve bags. They carry their briefs and other things in their bags and they leave them in a robing room when they are in court. There can be quite a lot of old bags in a robing room. This may be why solicitors are not meant to go into robing rooms, even to speak to the barrister dealing with their case. Solicitors are meant to use the solicitors' room at court. If such can be located, it will be less than eight feet square and will have a broken digital security lock (since no-one can remember the number and they had to get in somehow).

When in court, barristers sit in front and solicitors sit behind. Clients can sit anywhere else as long as they shut up and do not think they have any relevance to the proceedings. In very important cases there may be two barristers for the client and the senior one will be a silk (see Queen's Counsel). The solicitor sits in the very front where the judge can keep a better eye on him. The very important barrister sits behind the solicitor and the less important barrister sits behind them. There isn't much room for the client, but in that sort of a case he or she would be better off at work trying to earn enough to pay for all three lawyers anyway.

Queen's Counsel

Queen's counsel are posers. They are barristers who have tired of the ordinary gown and who have said: "Stuff it, I want a silk one." This is why the junior barrister's gown is called a stuff gown and the senior one gets to wear a silk gown. They also sport a fancy line in black waistcoats. Q.C.s get paid a huge amount of money and have a lot of the work done for them by a junior barrister who has to be instructed at the same time.

Most Q.C.s are mega clever and have thought processes which start where ordinary mortals leave off. They tend to crack jokes in Latin and use fancy words like 'adumbrate' which makes them popular with intellectual judges who still have not heard of the Beatles.

Prospective Q.C.s have to apply to the Lord Chancellor who has minions who decide whether or not to make the appointment. If the Q.C. has not kept his nose clean, or does not know enough rude Latin jokes, he stays a junior. The appointment process is meant to be a deep dark secret so that other lawyers can speak freely without offending the applicant. But the press have decided the process needs to be more open, which probably means that no-one will say anything to anybody let alone the Lord Chancellor's department. This means that lots of duffers will get appointed. The press will say that all lawyers are duffers anyway. The press do not like lawyers since they get in the way of a good story by trying to uncover the truth.

Eventually Q.C.s get to be poor again because they are asked to be Judges and have to accept. This means their income goes down from over £500,000 a year to about £70,000 a year – all for the privilege of wearing a coloured dressing gown, a smaller wig, and being called 'Your Honour', 'Your Lordship', or 'My Lord'. This proves the 'Q.C.s are posers' theory to be correct.

Judges

There are many different sorts of judges. Some are not very clever and get a rough ride from the press for rewarding rapists. Others are fine in the brain department but a bit pedestrian and awfully boring at cocktail parties. Some are incredibly whiz bang clever by which time they are usually 88 years old and forced to retire. Although the elderly whiz bang clever ones look just like your grandad and granny, appearances are deceptive. After they have been carried into court and had their wigs straightened they reveal the analytical brain of Einstein, the destructive power of Hiroshima and the patter of an educated Ben Elton with the rude bits taken out.

Learner judges are called Assistant Recorders which means they have to write everything down as they go along. This does not help to hurry cases along and is the reason why witnesses are often told to "speak at the speed of his lordship's pen". If learner recorders learn to write fast enough they become real Recorders and finally Circuit Judges. Circuit Judges are so called because they often go round and round in circles.

Most judges are pretty good, but in the lower Criminal courts and County courts there are a handful of not very clever ones because they were appointed from not very clever barristers or solicitors who were never going to be high flyers but liked the thought of the inflation-proofed pension.

The Civil High Court judges are usually the bright ones, and the best go on to be Appeal Court Judges who play in teams of three and wear a different coloured strip. Any barrister who tries to make anything less than a fantastically brilliant point to the Court of Appeal gets kicked in the shins by one of the three and then mugged by the other two before he can straighten up. This speeds up the cases no end.

Mega brilliant whiz bang crackerjack Appeal Court Judges get to be judges in the House of Lords. They are like school prefects since they do not have to wear a red dressing gown but can turn up in their ordinary suits. Of course, the barristers still have to wear their wigs and stuff which makes them look even more silly than in an ordinary court. They have a court in the House of Lords which is cunningly designed to have the worst acoustics in the Western Hemisphere so only those at the front have any idea what is going on. You do get a nice view of the Thames.

Then there are District Judges. No one much wanted to be one of them because they used to be called Registrars and if you said to your friends you were a Registrar they thought you were in Births and Deaths and Marriages and all that. So the LCD (Lord Chancellor's Department) thought up the clever wheeze of changing the name of Registrars to 'District Judges' and then lots and lots of people wanted to be one because people at cocktail parties cannot tell the difference and they all think you are a proper one. Also your wife gets a quick thrill out of people thinking she is a real judge's wife and being asked to give prizes for home-made jam at garden fêtes and things.

The latest trend is to advertise jobs for judges in the newspapers. Apparently the idea is to make it open to all. This is a bit difficult as the small print says you have to have been an Assistant Recorder or a Deputy District Judge to apply. To be one of those you have to have been a qualified barrister or solicitor of umpteen years' standing, with all sorts of relevant experience. So don't start trying on your wig in the bedroom mirror just yet.

The only good news is that if you are female and/or physically challenged and did not go to Eton (or any other public school) you will go to the top of the list. This is because the judiciary has to be balanced (not mentally). Since there are now more women than men becoming lawyers this will all change in about fifty years' time. Advertisements for politically incorrect ex-boarding school judges will then be choice of the day.

Stipendiary Magistrates

You cannot pose half as well as a stipe. Stipendiary magistrates, as you are meant to call them, sit on a bench (well it's a chair really, but you are meant to call it a bench) and substitute for a whole flock of magistrates (and you are meant to call them a bench of magistrates but they are much more like sheep).

The stipe is legally qualified and belts through more

cases before the mid-morning coffee than most lay magistrates do in a week. This is mainly because ordinary magistrates have to 'retire' to decide what they are going to do with the accused and drink coffee. Then they need to retire to go to the loo and drink more coffee, so the morning's work can take a lot of retirements. Also lay magistrates do not know anything much about the law (and lots of lawyers will say that they do not actually know anything much about anything) so they have to have a legally qualified clerk to tell them what they can, and more often what they cannot, do.

Chairmen of Industrial Tribunals

Improve your skills by listening in on an industrial tribunal. Everyone will think you are from the press and keep their distance, especially if you have a notebook and ask the lawyers for their names as they are going out of the door.

There will be three people trying to look busy on the top table. On one side is the flanker from the workers' side, usually a union official who will think he is a man of the people. The other flanker will be from the bosses' side, usually from some employers' federation or other (because employers who are actually in business are too busy trying to make money).

Do not expect too much of the flankers; they may not live in the real world and if they ask a question everyone will try to humour them by telling them what they think they want to hear. It is the one in the middle that you have to watch out for; he is the Chairman and, not only that, he is legally qualified. Avoid speculating out loud as to which legal system admitted him and on what basis.

Industrial Tribunal Chairmen try to be helpful; this is rarely a good thing. For a start, they will want the lawyer to speak sitting down when everyone knows lawyers are incapable of logical thought unless they are on their feet, so this will get things off to a bad start. Then the Chairman will lean over backwards so far to help the applicant (who is rarely represented) that the employer client gets angry, which is just what the Chairman wanted in the first place.

When it comes to giving judgment, the Chairman will probably dictate it into a strategically placed tape recorder in the hope that any loud expletives uttered by the employer or his lawyer can be recorded for future disciplinary action. The judgment will anticipate every likely ground of appeal and be structured in such a way as to close off each avenue.

Academic Lawyers

This species dresses colourfully and lives on inadequate salaries in old and crumbling buildings. These dwellings are called law faculties. The male can often be identified by his beard. Groups of academic lawyers often gather at watering holes called seminars. They usually migrate in the summer months.

A characteristic of the breed is a suspicion of lawyers in private practice. This suspicion is fuelled by the outdated belief that such lawyers are rich and drive expensive motor cars.

Due to the process of evolution academic lawyers are developing changed feeding habits. These 'rich pickings' (as they are commonly known) arise from the training of their young. To share in these pickings the academic lawyer has developed an unexpected interest in life outside the nest. This unfamiliar terrain contains sometimes benign but ultimately dangerous predators such as 'market forces'. Experienced observers believe the academic's inexperience in this new territory may have tragic consequences for long term survival. Others argue that other lawyer species whose traditional food supplies are dwindling should supplement their stocks by joining the fledgling training scheme. This could lead to an even greater over-supply of young lawyers and threaten the balance of the ecology.

In-house Lawyers

This grey suited, well insured and fully-pensioned form of lawyer was generally considered to have a retiring disposition, little inclination for travel and to occupy modest but comfortable corners within the open plan areas of very large company habitats. In recent years the more forceful members have developed greatly changed habits. These include brighter camouflage, an enthusiasm for first class travel, and highly decorated and ever larger lairs. These evolutionary Creatures take up residence within mega companies (or those with mega legal problems) but often revert to their original customs by continuing to seek legal advice from outside private practice.

Some private practice lawyers used to be disdainful of the civilized routines of the in-house kind by drawing unflattering comparisons with what they called the excitement and potential of private practice.

However some keen observers of the new variety have now totted up the value to the in-house specimen of the boring regular salary, boring car, boring company pension scheme, boring life insurance, boring medical cover, boringly long holidays, boring bonus and the odd boring share option. Those observers suggest that the excitement to the private practitioner of having unlimited personal liability and of having to borrow over £100,000 to fund the firm's office account is beginning to pall. They believe that when this is set against flying Club Class for a one and only employer company client, with freedom to delegate all the tricky bits to external solicitors or counsel, more people may seek to emulate their lifestyle.

In particular, they believe that the best part may be the thrill of forcing the private practitioners to parade their services, to make them jump through all sorts of hoops to get the work, and to then beat them down to a pittance on price.

Crown Prosecutors

Never repeat out loud that Police Inspectors used to do the job of Crown Prosecution Service lawyers splendidly in olden times.

Instead commiserate about how sad it must be not to be a proper lawyer with the potential to be filthy rich, jetting about the place representing mega private clients or name-dropped multi-nationals, but be careful about doing so at ten o'clock of a wet Tuesday morning within earshot of a bags-under-the-eyes real life been-at-the-police-station-on-legal-aid-rates-all-night defence solicitor from provincial private practice.

Perhaps the CPS may not be the job for the power-seeking high-flyer but nonetheless it's a modest little earner for those waiting for the glut in the profession to fade away or for the lawyer housemother returning to the earnings fold. Particularly as when they forget the file (or the prisoner) they can blame the introduction of their new quality systems (or Group 4) and fade back into bureaucratic obscurity.

Local Authority Lawyers

In every town hall or local authority seat of power lurk clusters of lawyers. Brow beaten by political pressure and hardened by cynicism, these rumpled-suited legal luminaries are armour plated against the pressures of time. Deprived of funds to employ sufficient numbers in their departments because of the more pressing needs of the Gay Druids Pensioners Action Group, they go more slowly than a Spanish labourer during his siesta.

Sometimes courteous, usually overworked, reluctant to reach decisions, and incapable of responding to correspondence in less than six weeks, they should be treated with compassion.

Legal Executives

Legal Executives were once called Managing Clerks before the word 'clerk' lost its standing.

All aspiring lawyers should curry favour with Legal Executives. They are the very sort your Mother always hoped you would marry. Solid, sober (most of them), dependable, and well skilled in their field. The sort who wash their cars on Sunday mornings, have worked their way up through a firm from doing the photo-copying, and have proved to be the mainstay of the practice.

Still exploited in many firms where they labour for a

pittance and increase the partners' profits no end, many legal executives have suddenly appreciated their true worth. Some of them actually require payment at the going rate for the job. A few have become licensed conveyancers which also means they can charge you a fee for swearing at them.

Trainees

Trainee solicitors used to be called Articled Clerks and were required to sign 'Articles' – promising to be sober and diligent. Sobriety being less fashionable nowadays, present day Articles stick to the diligence bit and are now called 'trainee solicitors'.

Once upon a time the articled clerk was taught the theory of law at college and arrived at a solicitor's office to be taught how to apply that theory in practical legal life. It was acknowledged that solicitors who qualified donkey's years ago were much too out-of-date to teach legal theory but rather good at teaching the sneaky practicalities of the law in action.

Today's would-be solicitors are required to pay huge sums of money to academic institutions who pretend to teach them the practicalities which the academic lawyers never knew in the first place. It means that the trainees have insufficient time to learn the theory of law. This is called progress.

Everyone knows that solicitors are filthy rich and short of things on which to spend their money. This is good as they are now required to spend lots and lots of money sending trainees away on compulsory and very expensive courses to learn all the legal theory they should have been taught in the first place. If the trainee gets 22 days holiday a year and also has to go on 32 days' worth of expensive courses a year, then there will be less time for them to make mistakes in the office. Some numerate lawyers may be sufficiently good at arithmetic to realise that since there are only two hundred and something working days in a year the trainee will be on paid holiday or training for over a quarter of the time.

Trainee barristers are called 'pupils'. They have to find a 'set' to give them a pupillage. This is as tricky as finding a poor Q.C., but if they are incredibly lucky and get over that hurdle they will find themselves attached to a pupil master. This means that they do all the research work and drafting for a particular barrister – some pupils reckon slave master would be a more accurate description. The trainee barrister also has to eat dinners; trainee solicitors can rarely afford to eat.

Other Dramatis Legal Personae

Magistrates

The majority of magistrates are public spirited, competent and well meaning, and no-more given to bizarre judgments than a Circuit judge. One or two treat their appointment as divine intervention, cease the consumption of alcohol, and eliminate those endearing human attributes that made them suitable for appointment in the first place. Others are self seeking and prone to have their wrists slapped for such earth shattering acts of self aggrandisement as signing themselves 'Justice of the Peace'.

Magistrates usually sit in threes. The magistrate in the middle gets to sit in a big chair (sorry, bench) and is encouraged to preach to the accused just like preaching from a pulpit in the church but with more emphasis on morality. Much of the dramatic effect of the chairman of the bench's sermon is spoilt by his being reminded by the clerk to read formal warnings chosen from a sort of prayer book issued by the Lord Chancellor's department. When this happens everyone's eyes glaze over so some magistrates choose to liven things up by reading out the wrong bit or pretending dyslexic disfunction.

The morale, status and value of magistrates would be improved by restoring a bit of flagellation (of the accused, not the magistrates). All magistrates like to see a bit of quivering and trembling amongst the accused. Nowadays this usually results from suppressed laughter.

The idea behind the magisterial system is that one should be judged by one's peers. Solicitors think this is why the Lord Chancellor sits in the House of Lords.

Magistrates' Clerks

The ferocity of the average magistrate's clerk is increased by their seniority and by the importance of the court in which they are sitting. Occupying a bench of their own just below that of the Magistrates, clerks are there to terrorise the accused and the young lawyer in equal measure whilst keeping the magistrates on a tight leash (and occasionally a choke chain).

A good deal of entertainment may be had from observing the clerk's skill in remaining awake and passably controlled despite being confronted with an endless diet of routine trivia, inept advocacy, often bizarre decisions and limited powers of retribution.

The true test of experienced advocates is their ability to ingratiate themselves with the clerk and thereby jump their case to the top of the list, whilst remaining on reasonable terms with legal brethren waiting their turn. The advocates' cultivation of the clerk can be their passport to escaping the confines of the court.

Barristers' Clerks

The Barrister's Clerk is the wheeling, dealing, power behind the throne, first-second-and-third-line-of-defence to, and source of funds for, all the barristers within the clerk's chambers.

Take a set of London Chambers, five Q.C.s earning over a quarter of a million apiece, fifteen barristers at £100K each, cream off 10% commission, deduct office expenses, and buy that little yacht in the Med. It is not quite as good as that these days, and not so great outside the metropolis, but still worth consideration if you do not mind a few years of wheeling wire trolleys full of reference books across the Strand.

Solicitors NEVER TALK TO BARRISTERS ABOUT MONEY. To do so will risk incurring the pent-up wrath of purple-faced counsel and the explosive indignation of their clerks.

All negotiations about what the barrister is to be paid are conducted through the clerk. Be sure he will hit the solicitor when his defences are at their lowest, usually around 4.15 pm on the worst day of the solicitor's life (worst days of their life occur on average five times a week) when they are shouting into two telephones, have a queue of secretaries and trainees waiting at their desk, the computer network has gone down, their clients have been in the waiting room for an hour and they have four deadlines to meet before the 7 p.m. partners' meeting. This is the moment at which 'John' will be on the phone, deferentially reminding the solicitor of the need to fix a fee for Mr. Marshall Hall's appearance in the morning. "It's a day out of his life, sir; and he's been preparing for five days. Shall we say £7,000 for the Brief and £4,000 for the Refresher?"

Barristers' clerks train for negotiation by knocking out nuclear arms treaties before breakfast. By leaving the deal to the last moment they put themselves in the driving seat (with a big whip), leaving the solicitor over a barrel because there is not enough time to pull back the brief and give it to someone else. Also in big cases where the negotiation can be months in advance there will be talk of money up front, stage payments and other ploys.

Solicitors get some satisfaction from the tradition of calling all clerks by their christian names and having them reply 'Sir', but learn to wave deferentially on holiday when their rubber dinghy is swamped by the barrister's clerk's forty-footer.

Ushers

The Usher wears a gown and stands at the door of the court – counting them all in and counting them all out. Of great importance to county court advocates, it is the usher who usually controls the order in which cases are called.

Bonhomie or even offers of alcoholic reward should re-order the list. Lawyers should save their effort in magistrates courts since few ushers have that influence and it is certainly not worth attempting to bribe the clerk in lieu. Ushing could be a nice little earner for bored bluffers or vacuous retired observers of human frailty.

The Lawyers' Trade Unions

The Law Society

The Law Society is the solicitors' governing body and in order to get a certificate to practise, all solicitors must pay an annual fee. This costs them around £500 each for starters but only raises thirty million or so a year which does not go far towards having real fun.

To make it a bit more worthwhile, the Society requires all solicitors who advise someone's granny on investing her money to pay another subscription to hold an 'Investment Business Certificate'. This raises more millions to keep the gravy train going.

An even better scheme has been for the Law Society to get any solicitors who think they are any good in a particular area (such as planning, or personal injury) to pass an exam so they can pay yet another subscription to be allowed to call themselves a 'specialist'. This raises even more money.

But most of the Society's satisfaction comes from requiring the solicitors to pay around £10,000 plus per partner for professional indemnity insurance, and just when this has been extracted, the coup de grâce is delivered – a reminder about the 'Compensation fund'. This hovers around a thousand pounds per lawyer per year to repay anyone in the world who loses money through the activities of a small proportion of fraudulent solicitors. Most of this levy goes to banks and building societies who think lawyers are complete mugs for having such a scheme, but cry foul instantly if abolition is proposed.

It is bad manners to speculate about whether the supply of specialities, fees and levies will keep the Society going for long enough to restore its premises to a standard of opulence worthy of the Palace of Versailles. When next in the area, pay a visit to the Law Society's Hall in Chancery Lane. Say you are down from the provinces – you have forgotten your I.D. card and confidently turn right at the hall porter, park your umbrella, and you will find the wine bar to the right and straight ahead big leather armchairs to fall asleep in.

Subscriptions to the Law Society also pay for the OSS, initials which stand for the Office for the Supervision of Solicitors and are sufficient to strike dread into the heart of any busy practitioner. Not only does the OSS investigate complaints, but it also insists on solicitors telling all their clients about it at every convenient opportunity. This keeps the work flowing in.

At least once every year the OSS holds a press conference to tell everyone how negligent solicitors really are. This is like paying a subscription to buy the cartridges to shoot yourself in the foot. It is thought to improve the image of the profession no end.

The Bar Council

The Bar Council is smaller and charges less money but then there are not that many barristers around. Also they do not handle money so they do not get the chance to defraud anyone which means that there is no levy.

There is, however, dangerous talk of complaints procedures and compensation having to be paid by incompetent barristers. How ridiculous – barristers are perfect and never make mistakes – ask one.

Both the Law Society and the Bar Council run the disciplinary tribunals which can strike the lawyer off if he or she steps out of line. Whether or not the line is drawn closely enough, what constitutes stepping over it rather than on it, and what scale of punishment is appropriate for being critical about these two institutions, are all issues upon which no lawyers would wish to be drawn for fear of being struck off.

Legal Aid

The Legal Aid Act 1988 bravely declares its purpose as the production of a publicly funded framework to provide advice to people 'who might otherwise be unable to obtain it on account of their means'.

The trouble is that the government decides what 'means' means. In parallel with raising eligibility to a level which is completely out of reach of most 'ordinary' people, the civil court rules have been changed to intensify the work needed to be done before trial. This means that legal costs have increased, which in turn allows the Lord Chancellor to argue that it is all the fault of the lawyers and to cut legal aid costs rates to show them who's in charge. Now fixed fees, block contracts, franchises, and abandonment of legal aid for Conditional Fee Agreements rule the day so the days of the civil legal aid certificate yielding a miniscule profit are numbered.

Remember that there is civil legal aid and criminal legal aid and that it is incredibly difficult to get the first and dead easy to get the second – especially if you are a foreign millionaire or have done something particularly heinous (and intend to lie through your teeth and deny everything to put up the cost of the trial).

To bluff your way around the legal aid system you need to know there are Green forms, emergency certificates, limited certificates, full certificates and ABWOR. Talk casually of ABWOR and your credibility is assured. Even if you tell your friends it stands for Assistance By Way of Representation, they will be none the wiser.

The Clients

Clients and their problems come in different shapes and sizes. Some clients can be unsporting and bring in cases which overlap more than one area of law; this can be confusing but the difficulty will often be overcome by the word 'focussing'. In giving advice, focus on the main problem which will be the only one you can remember anything about. By constantly talking of this focus you may distract them from other areas in which you are less certain.

It is helpful to know that private (as opposed to business) clients tend to fall into well defined anthropological or sociological categories some of which are summarised as follows:

Suspicious – Believes the lawyer's purpose in life is to overcharge for inadequate advice. Checks watch on arrival and departure. Constantly tries to catch the lawyer out. Insists on every sub-clause being explained in enormous detail and then queries any time charged for this process. Challenges any advice given by quoting contrary view of anonymous legally qualified friend. Scrutinises bill with fanaticism. Incapable of being satisfied. Advice: avoid if possible.

Malleable – Smiles vacantly at whatever advice is given. Expects the lawyer to decide everything. Incapable of decisive thought. Has the listening power of a dead parrot. Responds to all questions "I'll leave it all to you to decide, after all you know best". Tends to forget all advice given once things go wrong. Advice: watch your back at all times.

Emotional – Weeps at first interview. Permanently downtrodden by vagaries of life. Occasionally lightens gloom with brave, watery smile. Needs permanent injection of backbone but resists all lawyer's efforts to strengthen resolve. Advice: buy more tissues.

Aggressive – Spends life bullying others and is not going to stop now. Demands action, rejects unpalatable advice. "Now you look here, I'm paying you to do this..." Needs to be shouted down, may respect lawyer for it, but more likely to offer violence and move elsewhere. Usually married to 'emotional' wife. Advice: for lawyers who like a challenge.

Litigious – Believes letters are for cowards. Has motto: "If it moves, sue it." Once won a case (more by luck than merit) and believes the world is now his/her legal oyster. Has had sixteen previous firms of lawyers and is suing all of them. Flatters your ego to persuade you to take latest case and then reveals true colours. Advice: check indemnity insurance policy.

Conspiratorial – Seeks to draw lawyer into web of intrigue. Cannot understand concepts of integrity or duty to court. Tells lawyer everything he intends to conceal from the court and is astounded at any reluctance to become co-plotter. Subscribes to conspiracy theory of life and believes the bench is as bent as he is. Advice: send down the road to your least favourite competitor.

Over-friendly – Develops crush on lawyer. Displays similar tendencies with doctor and vicar. Writes on scented notepaper, sends presents and suggests home consultations. Requires sole attention of object of desire. Rings frequently. Seeks help with completing forms, calling the plumber and changing the fuse. Advice: keep at arm's length (or seek a large legacy).

Obsessive – Arrives shortly after an unfortunate aroma. Carries worldly possessions in a plastic bag. Ricochets from lawyer to doctor to social services to citizens advice bureau. Prone to abandoning empty wine bottles in the reception area. Bounced as often as a Wimbledon tennis ball. Advice: send largest trainee solicitor to reception office to sort out.

Meticulous – Requires lawyer to absorb entire life history before giving the simplest advice. Resists all attempts to short circuit recitation of irrelevant facts. Obsessive as to detail. Encyclopædic knowledge of facts of the case. Corrects lawyer's minutest error. Client's tedium is matched only by indignation at the delivery of bill based on time spent. Advice: delegate to eager trainee to take statement.

Perfect – Responds promptly to all communications. Listens to advice and does what is told. Anticipates requests for information by producing precise type-written lists. Understands explanations. Displays appreciation for efforts. Pays bill promptly and sends whisky or flowers to emphasize thanks. Advice: treasure, another may not pass your way again.

THE LAW ITSELF

Researching the Law

It is not what you know that is important. It is knowing where you can look it up. Unfortunately, for most law books you need a degree in philosophy, nuclear physics and higher mathematics to understand the index.

Nowadays most law volumes come in what the publishers call 'loose leaf format'. Contrary to what you would expect, this is not just to ensure that the book will always be up-to-date. It is a cunning device to extort an extra £250 out of the lawyer for each year from now until doomsday. These payments, in exchange for which one receives a vacuum sealed pack of random paper at six monthly intervals, so cripple the legal customer that after a short while he or she cancels the order for this annual 'noter-up' and in consequence the book soon becomes of historical importance only.

The other modern trend is for the index to live in a separate volume to the text. You will find that the index volume goes missing as a matter of routine, thus rendering the entire publication useless. Now a new scam looms – books are on CD Rom or disc so that you can interact with the index (which sounds nothing like as enjoyable as interacting with a shapely librarian). So is this cheaper? Not on your life: you are charged a higher price and you will also pay much more for the inevitable updates. All this will probably mean that only groups of two or three hundred lawyers together will be able to afford more than a tiny library. As a result lawyers will have to become specialists because they cannot afford enough current books or CDs to be generalists.

Most law reports and law works are now on computer databases. Intranets, Internets and CD Rom juke boxes of hypertext data proliferate and make a mind-boggling volume of law available at an ever increasing price. Not that any lawyer ever has time to read them, but carrying the laptop into court lets them play Patience when boredom sets in.

Trainee solicitors represent the traditional way of researching law. The price of progress is the difference between a square jawed pre-Luddite trainee and a square screened post-technological display monitor. Under the traditional system the solicitor scribbles an illegible request on the back of an envelope. The trainee instantly divines the precise point the solicitor had in mind and writes a ten page exposition quoting all known case law on the subject.

It is no different in the brave new world of information technology: ask the wrong question and you will still get a long answer. It does not much matter because the client will still refuse to pay for the research on the basis that all lawyers should know all the law all of the time anyway.

Criminal Law

Criminal law is pretty straightforward so a bluffer can be at a disadvantage. To complicate things as much as possible try to concentrate on three areas.

1) Evidence. Lecturers in law are apt to make turgid pronouncements such as 'judicial evidence divides between direct or circumstantial evidence and primary and secondary evidence'. This probably has something

to do with the joys of hearsay evidence, corroboration and the competence and compellability of witnesses. It used to be the case that most sane adults were both competent and compellable but then there was a lot of argument as to whether or not wives were competent or compellable, or both (or sometimes neither) which all caused a certain amount of ill feeling, and is a subject you might seek to avoid. The best policy is to talk loftily of privilege, prejudice and inadmissibility and the listeners' eyes will probably glaze over.

More fertile ground for bluffers is:

2) *'mens rea'* – not a misspelling of the male posterior, but Latin for something to do with his thought processes.

The great idea is that if the accused pours enough lager and vodka and lime down his throat, to the extent that he does not know what he is doing, he may get let off. This is why 90% of the male population spends its time pickling its brains. It's what is called taking precautions. There is also *'actus rea'* – which is more straightforward until you consider the maxim *'actus non facit reum, nisi mens sit rea'* which confuses people no end. Much more important is:

3) The 'Standard of Proof'. If you remember nothing else, drum into your mind that the standard of proof in criminal law is 'beyond reasonable doubt', whereas in civil cases it is only 'on the balance of probabilities'. Some solicitors are believed to have qualified on the basis of that knowledge alone.

All criminal cases start in a magistrates court which has what is called 'summary' jurisdiction. Less serious cases stay there, but really naughty people get to be tried 'on indictment' by the Crown court. Some offences

41

are triable either way. This is not a glancing reference to sexual orientation but the right to choose to be tried by either a bunch (sorry, bench) of magistrates or before a Crown court jury who may be bamboozled more easily. The jury only decides guilt or innocence and does not pass sentence. Sentencing can be likened to an art form. Like most modern art few people understand it and all you need to remember is that common sense should be ignored at all costs.

Civil Law

This concerns civil wrongs, property and succession and a whole host of sub-divisions. Contract is a good place to start.

The Law of Contract

It may seem odd, but the old continental system of contract was called 'laissez faire' which is French for the exact opposite of what the European courts stand for today. Enthusiasts will know that in present day contract law you need to stir in four ingredients namely: Offer, Acceptance, Consideration and an Intention to create Relations. The case of a lawyer called Angus Diggle demonstrated the importance of not mixing these up.

The Offer can be made to the public at large – as did the Carbolic Company with its incredible smoking balls (they advertised that if you lit one up you would not catch cold – it did not work, but the court action did). An Offer must consist of a definite promise to be bound (which may appeal to bondage fetishists) and there are special provisions about exhibiting yourself in shops. As a rule, death terminates an Offer (which is bad news for necrophiliacs).

There is not much to say about Acceptance save that silence is rarely sufficient. Endless argument can be caused by claiming correctly that two identical Offers will not usually constitute an Acceptance if they cross in the post.

Consideration may look like money but in reality has mysterious powers of movement towards the person making the promise and is best avoided in polite conversation.

If you wish to stop the conversation stone dead, you may care to refer to *'quasi-equitable estoppel'* in this context. You have only to memorise the shortened explanation. For instance, that this occurs in the absence of Consideration when a promise not to insist upon a claim is made – which the promisor intends to create legal relations and which he intends to be acted upon by the promisee – and on which the promisee does in fact act so the promise may be used by the promisee as a defence to any action brought against him on the original claim but it is not a true case of estoppel because there is no misrepresentation of an existing fact. All this was the fault of Mr. Justice Denning (as he then was) who invented the whole thing to make sure he got his own way (which he always did).

Contracts are full of express terms (which are no faster than terms sent by second class post) and implied terms except that the implied terms are not actually in the contract so you make them up as you go along. Once you have sorted that lot out you get to Mistake, Misrepresentation, Duress and Undue Influence, not to mention the differences between

Innocent Misrepresentation and Fraudulent Misrepresentation and whether or not you can force the pace with a touch of Specific Performance. Those who find all this confusing will delight in the doctrine of Frustration which should be put to music and sung to the tune of that famous Rolling Stones song about the inability to obtain satisfaction.

One of the greatest joys in contract law is rescission. If you rescind the contract it gets you back to where you started, which can be rather useful. Sadly you usually have to make up your mind between rescission and damages; also, rescission is like sex in the office, it usually has to be done rather quickly.

Latin gets into contract law quite often. The best phrase is *caveat emptor* which means it was the individual's own silly fault for buying whatever it was in the first place.

The law of contract is relatively straightforward overall, as long as you are not suffering from disability. Disability is a definite disadvantage in contract. Even perfectly hale and hearty seventeen year-olds suffer from it as a matter of course and used to be lumped together with such other more obviously disabled persons as those of unsound mind, drunkards and married women. In fact married women miraculously and simultaneously overcame most of their disabilities with the granting of the Married Women (Restraint upon Anticipation) Act 1949. It is believed that this has now come into force.

The Law of Tort

If it is not a broken contract or broken trust then it is usually a tort. In Germany a tort has an 'e' on the end and consists of a sticky cake which squirts cream all over you when you try to eat it. Tort can also bring you to a sticky end but until publication of an EU directive to the contrary a tort in England is a sort of civil wrong. To get any dosh by way of damages for a tort, as a general rule someone has to be to blame. It is not enough to be injured, someone somewhere has to have done something wrong.

Of course, doing something wrong may also mean that, as well as a tort, it's a crime, or even a breach of contract. It can clearly be seen that this gives plenty of scope for arguing lots of alternative complications. Complications mean costs, which is why lawyers encourage them. Divine intervention also gets a look in: in those few cases where none needs to be to blame (called strict liability), an Act of God can be a good defence – although calling Him as a witness does present certain technical problems.

There are all sorts of torts, and every now and then a new one gets invented. Trespass is always good for a bit of fun: you can do it to persons, to goods, to land and arguably to all three at the same time. Nuisance is even better, you can do it in private or in public and there are some delightfully infuriating rules. For example, one can dine out on the rule that it is no defence that the claimant knew all about the nuisance in advance. This means that you can move into a house bang next door to the noisiest factory in England, and sue for nuisance before the hangover from your house-warming party has worn off.

Then there is defamation and malicious falsehood. Defamation covers slander and libel – the first, of course, being spoken and the second written. Be suitably disdainful when people mix them up, while knowing that as multi-media computer output increases the two are bound to get mixed up and lots of lovely lawyers' fees can be spent trying to decide which is which.

A great bonus is that goods can be slandered just as well as individuals, but in either case a good measure of malice or recklessness is important. Those traditional defences of 'justification' and 'fair comment' are the best because in proving them one way or the other the poor old plaintiff gets far more adverse publicity than would ever have been possible by ignoring the whole thing in the first place. So, after lawyers are paid £100,000 for defending a good name, the press ensures that it gets dragged through the mud.

Nowadays in defamation cases you do not see so much of the good old defence that the words used were: 'mere vulgar abuse'. This is because everyone has become so vulgar that no-one notices.

It is worth remembering two more things about defamation. The first is that you cannot get legal aid for it, which may be sad for the lawyers but good for the peace of the world. The second is that you will probably appear in front of a jury and (which is far worse) the jury is allowed to choose the level of damages. In America, juries fix damages all the time which is why you get such foolishly large awards there. Juries in civil cases are very rare in England but when they are used you get equally foolish awards. The beauty of a jury is that no-one has the slightest idea what the claim is worth until mega-bucks have been spent taking the case all the way to court. Quite a lot of lawyers are in favour of juries. If nothing else, it gives them a bigger audience for posing to.

There are lots more torts including breach of copyright, and passing off, but the biggest and most abundant is negligence. Every time there is a crash on the road, a collision at sea, an accident at work or in the home, the surgeon saws off the wrong leg, the factory fails to screw a toaster together properly, a football stand or a building collapses – negligence rears its head. Without the tort of negligence the insurance industry would grind to a halt, the armies of expert witnesses and forensic accountants would be thrown out of work, the court system would not know what to do with itself and the legal system would collapse.

A smattering of knowledge of negligence is thus a necessary adjunct to your armoury, for which purpose a short glossary may suffice:

Neighbour – Not the person you ogle over the garden fence but someone to whom you owe a duty of care.

Duty of care – Avoiding being bloody stupid.

Breach of duty of care – Being bloody stupid.

Reasonable foreseeability – Being bright enough to identify the person who is about to be injured by your being bloody stupid.

Contributory negligence – Injuring others who are themselves being bloody stupid (which they must be because they will lose part of their damages).

Donoghue and Stevenson – A very important case of a snail in a stone ginger beer bottle as a result of which Lord Atkin gave a rather nifty definition of who a neighbour really is.

Tripper – Not someone off to the seaside, but a claimant who falls foul of a paving slab.

Occupier – A bit of a liability.

Insurer – Someone who is trained to find ways of showing that negligence never happened.

Res ipsa loquitur – An anthropological phenomenon whereby facts give tongue.

Rylands and Fletcher – Another very important case which says if people collect dangerous things for a hobby they may get into trouble.

Visitors – People not to have round if you are unwise enough to be an occupier.

Volenti non fit injuria – Latin for saying it's your own silly fault for having been there in the first place.

In summary, negligence is like a fertility drug, the more of it you have, the more lawyers are produced.

The Law of Partnership

This defines the relationship between persons carrying on a business in common with a view to profit. Note the words: 'with a view to...' This is the trouble. Partnerships start with boundless enthusiasm and with the expectation of making money. If they succeed then, as sure as eggs is eggs, one partner will find a way of making off with the lion's share of the lolly and the inevitable dispute will centre around who should really have what.

On the other hand when, as is more often the case, the partnership loses money, the argument will rage over the liabilities or what is left of the assets. That brings you to the real joy of many partnership disputes – the total lack of any partnership deed or other evidence of what was intended.

A partnership agreement is said to be 'valid and enforceable without formalities and by mere word of mouth'. On this basis you had better be careful of your

reply to the invitation: 'let's you and me get together...?'
Fortunately, in partnership there is a duty of 'utmost good faith' to your partner or partners.

A short glossary on the subject may help:

Implied authority – The right of one partner to bind the other (see bondage).

Ostensible authority – The pretence that your partner will let you do something for yourself.

Interest on advances – Accepting an invitation to 'coffee at my place'.

Dissolution – About as helpful to partnerships as it was to the monasteries.

Taking an account – Spending a fortune on having someone calculate the little that is left following dissolution, so another fortune can then be spent arguing how to divide anything that remains.

Company Law

Company lawyers are complex creatures. Half the time they act out a frenetic existence, professing to be on the edge of a precipice, faxing 50-page takeover documents back and forth. They regard the length of takeover meetings as a measure of virility and consider any opposing lawyer who wants to reach completion in less than three continuous days and nights as a spineless wimp.

The other half of the time company lawyers bemoan the lack of corporate activity, bite their fingernails and speculate on an unsolicited career change. If they do find themselves seeking alternative employment they soon find that recruitment of company lawyers is based on SAS sleep deprivation techniques and knowledge of yellow books, blue books and other garishly coloured publications. Company lawyers like an inventive turn of phrase. Golden handshakes lead to golden goodbyes, golden hellos and golden handcuffs. Their inventiveness does not extend to naming new potential companies which are always called Newco.

Those who seek to impress in this field must first consider the attributes of a company. Registered companies can be limited by shares, by guarantees or by absolutely nothing at all. They can have ordinary shares, preference shares, debentures, and other riveting qualities. They also have meetings. Meetings involve giving notice, the length of which depends on resolution. This in turn depends on being ordinary or special and often turns on proxies. Proxies are bits of paper held by chairmen of company meetings to prevent any criticism of their conduct having the slightest effect.

People can get rather excited at company meetings which is when liquidators and receivers get in on the act. The great beauty of being one of those is that you can charge a percentage for getting in all the assets, a fee for looking after them for a few moments, and then another fee for paying them all out again.

Bankruptcy should not be confused with winding-up. Winding up is for companies (and clocks) but bankruptcy is for individuals. So are IVAs. It used to be the case that only government officials called Official Receivers would sort out people who went bankrupt, because there was not enough money left over for accountants to earn fat fees for acting as a 'Trustee in Bankruptcy'. Then they invented the IVA (Individual Voluntary Arrangement) which meant that the accountants could get in on the act and have some fees up front for staving off bankruptcies. Accountants acting as liquidators, receivers or trustees always have liabilities but it is most important for them also to have priorities. Priorities means they get their fees first.

Here is a short glossary on company law:

MBO – What your best friend never told you about management.

Member – Something you may want to keep hidden.

Shadow director – Someone connected with the company who is exposing himself.

Takeover – Something like a legover; best for the recipient to lie back and think of England until it is all over.

Flotation – A process which helps major shareholders launch their yachts.

Liquidity – The stuff that yachts float on.

Floating charges – Called mines in wartime; can explode and sink unsuspecting companies.

Chargeholder – Usually the bank who laid the mines in the first place.

Refinancing – A minesweeping operation where you can end up with one enormous mine instead of lots of smaller ones.

Family Law

Once upon a time boys and girls fell in love, married, produced a couple of lovely children, and lived happily ever after. In those days divorce was a matter of disgrace and only a so-called 'innocent' spouse could secure one. In the lifetime of most of England's present judges, a petitioner seeking a divorce decree had to hand to the judge a 'discretion statement' detailing any adultery of their own, and if they failed to disclose it a chap called the 'Queen's Proctor' was employed to try to prove otherwise. There was 'custody' and 'access' of children, money matters were decided by specialist lawyers after careful argument, and everyone knew that a spouse who had done wrong and left home for another partner would probably lose any right to be maintained.

The only survivor from this scenario is the Queen's Proctor, who still lurks in Whitehall, performing one knows not what arcane and mysterious duties. Custody has turned into 'Residence'; Access has metamorphosed into 'Contact'; maintenance is fixed by teams of fun-loving CSA unqualified clerks, and leaving home to commit adultery is no bar to anything at all, let alone financial. At least petitions for divorce still survive, now based on 'irretrievable breakdown of marriage'; they still subdivide into grounds of adultery, unreasonable behaviour and separation of one sort or another. It may be that 'unreasonable behaviour' has less impact than 'cruelty' but, whatever the name, hitting your spouse over the head with a frying pan at regular intervals is still frowned upon in some courts.

You need to avoid the trap, beloved of the media, of referring to 'quickie' divorces. For the last 20 years, 90% of all divorces have been dealt with by what was once called 'the quicker' method of filing of affidavits, but to imbue them with some mystique of speed confuses the public no end. Fully defended (slowie?) divorces are as rare as lawyers making a profit from legal aid.

Most of the fun in family law comes from dividing up the loot. Logic demands that where a family cannot survive financially sharing one home with one set of overheads, financial nirvana will rarely follow a division of that same household into two.

Most of what one needs to know about family law is included in the following:

Date of marriage – Something only a wife can remember.

Marriage vows – Promises for which the sell-by date has expired.

Petitioner – The spouse that gets to the solicitor first; the quickest on the draw.

Respondent – Spouse suffering from a phobia about long brown envelopes dropping through the letter-box.

Husband – Name for a particular sort of spouse who will be asked to pay all the legal costs.

Wife – Daughter of mother-in-law.

Child – Expensive investment worth retaining for Child Support Agency purposes.

Adultery – Doing unto others that which should have been done to a spouse.

In flagrante delicto – As above but in front of an unexpected audience.

Reconciliation – Realisation that even if the grass is greener on the other side it will be too expensive to lie on it.

Employment Law

In more feudal days this was called the Law of Master and Servant, an evocative description that suggested a degree of control by the former over the latter. All this changed with the advent of the Industrial Tribunal which dispelled any foolish thoughts that any employer had any rights over anyone, let alone an employee. In tribunal law both parties are equal, but employees are more equal than others.

Employment law has always been a political football. The original concept was that an industrial tribunal would be a simple and straightforward forum where claims could be sorted out without either complex laws or expensive lawyers being involved. Any bluffer with a talent for hollow laughter, should now recognise that this is the time to give voice. It is not simply the stupendous volume of industrial tribunal case law, employment appeal tribunal case law, and constant verbiage on the topic that surprises you, but the sheer banality of most of it. This is another area where European law adds its social irrelevancies to the glutinous mixture.

Not for the tribunals is the unctuous 'after you, Claude' atmosphere of the High Court. Within the corridors of the tribunals lurk the lizard lawyers of the employers rubbing shoulders with the unsmiling 'got-them-at-last' union officials. These jostle with the serried ranks of state sponsored enthusiastic representatives from rights centres, discrimination agencies and law centres. In turgid state sits the chairman and his flankers bestowing deferential reverence upon the hapless suitor.

Statistics demonstrate that huge numbers of cases settle before the hearing, for which may ACAS be

praised. Whilst applauding their conciliatory intervention the bluffer may reflect on the number of 'nuisance
value' settlements where the employer is simply
persuaded to offer slightly less than the minimum he
will be forced to spend on lawyers. As tribunals virtually
never order costs against unsuccessful applicants, this
is about as surprising as day preceding night.

The Law of Insurance

The textbooks will tell you that a contract of insurance
differs from a wager because the insured has what is
called an 'insurable interest' in the risk. Most people
realise that gambling can be cheaper and even more
worthwhile than claiming against insurers. It may be
helpful to regard an insurance company as akin to a
bookmaker and keep it firmly in mind that the punter
usually loses in the end.

The insurance companies' first line of defence is the
loss adjuster or claims assessor. Ostensibly appointed
to assess the value of the claim, this species revels in
the sort of obsessive detail believed by many to stem
from too early childhood toilet training. Once the previ-
ously healthy amount of the claim has been margin-
alised in this way, the baton is passed on to the insurer.
Trained in rejection techniques from the high chair, the
insurer subjects the claimant and his lawyer to an
investigation not unlike the Spanish Inquisition. Any
minimal delay in notification of the claim, or failure to
disclose some seemingly irrelevant obscurity, invites
the claim's instant rejection.

The bluffer must first remember that a contract of
insurance (unless for life assurance, accident or health
insurance) is a contract of indemnity. It means the

insured cannot recover more than the actual loss. This is rather like your maximum winnings in the National Lottery being restricted to winning back the price of your ticket. Although there are some exceptions to prove the rule they usually only benefit the insurer. Into this happy world of Indemnity come the other two of the three muses, namely Subrogation and Contribution. Subrogation is all about insurers standing in insured's shoes, which can be rather uncomfortable for the insured.

Even more uncomfortable is the insurer's right to demand repayment of any compromise of the claim that the insured may have been unwise enough to make. Contribution is designed to stop the insured benefiting from the nifty scheme of insuring the same thing twice over. Of course, even if you are unwise enough to give that a whirl it will not stop the insurers taking two sets of insurance premiums in the meantime.

Then there is Salvage and Reinstatement and finally Assignment and Transfer. Whilst the last two may sound like the same thing, they are not. Finally, a skilled bluffer may want to let slip that a policy of insurance is a 'chose in action' – few people know that.

The Law of Property

A subject that has its origins in the Domesday Book is not to be taken lightly. The only concern of the first time buyers with a 10% fixed term mortgage may be to have the conveyancing done at around the cost of plumbing-in their new washing machine, but conveyancing life may not be as simple as fitting a new jubilee clip. Even seemingly simple transfers of new houses have their pitfalls.

Bear in mind there are freehold and leasehold interests, there are shortholds and flying freeholds; business tenancies and Farm business tenancies, regulated tenancies and assured tenancies. Then reflect upon the rare beauty of local and national planning provisions, highway authorities and environmental considerations and, of course, the joys of land charges, registered charges, first second and third mortgagees, mortgagors and restrictive covenants.

For the basics remember that just as lunatics can be certified and uncertified, freehold land can be registered or unregistered, though unregistered land is becoming as rare as reticence in the Royal Family.

The evocative prose of the Deed drips with instant archaic nostalgia. Messuages and Tenements jostle with appurtenances and abstracts. Rods, roods and riparian rights march alongside poles and perches. Hectares and heretofores mingle with hereditaments and hereafters. Restrictive covenants warn of the terrible consequences of digging sand from your land, keeping a common alehouse, burning bricks, or keeping yachts or trailers on your forecourt.

Amidst all this delightful verbiage lurks the Charge: a Charge by way of legal mortgage, a general equitable Charge, or perhaps even a registered Charge. It all comes down to security. Security is something which someone else invariably gets over a property, so called because it takes away the owner's own security or peace of mind. Security, once given, is as rarely released as a Sicilian hostage: indeed, the bandit-like qualities of the bank or building society holding the security strengthens the parallel.

The act of conveyancing is relatively quick and simple, rather like the act of sex – it is the bits before and after that take time and cost the money. Nevertheless, the solicitor is expected to be delighted with costs of six times less than those of the vendor's estate agent who also took the commission on that nice insurance policy.

The Law of Inheritance

Bluffers should be very wary about dying without first seeking legal advice. Advertisements in the daily newspapers for preparing Wills may suggest that life, which (for the sake of identification only) includes death, is straightforward. Nothing could be further from the truth.

The easy bit is to remember that if you die leaving a will then you die testate, and a grant of probate enables your executor or trustee to dish out the family jewels in accordance with your directions. It follows that if you die without a Will you are (which means were) intestate and only a grant of Letters of Administration will allow your garden gnomes to be distributed in the order decreed by statute. In those happy circumstances (for the inland revenue) your spouse gets quite a lot but much of this depends on who else is around at the time in the way of issue, parents, brothers, sisters and the like.

Issue is a posh way of referring to 'children, grand-children and remoter lineal descendants'. Blood is extremely important at this stage, whole blood is definitely an advantage over half blood – in fact if you are only half blooded it is worth asking for a transfusion just in case, since half-blooded uncles and aunts can even get in on the act. If you are like Eleanor Rigby and cannot discover even a half-blooded great aunt to be going along with, then all your millions are going to be declared 'bona vacantia' which is not Latin for 'have a good holiday' but actually means the Crown, the Duchy of Lancaster or the Duke of Cornwall cops the lot (and quite how the Duke of Cornwall got his name on the list is unclear). It follows that a Will is a splendid thing to have around, which is why half the population does not bother to make one.

Suffice it to say that Wills must be in writing save that if you happen to be on 'actual military service' you may be liable to make a nuncupative Will which can be oral – be wary of making jokes about your wordly wealth in the heat of battle.

Of course, the person making the Will (called either testator or testatrix according to testosterone level) has to be of 'testamentary capacity' which, being defined as 'a sound and disposing mind and memory', ensures that quite a few of the population fall at the first hurdle. Perhaps this is the advantage of doing it all by post – no-one will ever know.

You may find it useful to know that it is not a problem if you happen to be suffering from insane delusions, for as recently as 1826 the case of Dew v. Clark established that being pursued by evil spirits was fine, just as long as you still knew what a Will looked like at the time.

This is not the place to go into all the technicalities of wording, executing, and witnessing Wills, nor all the fun of revocation (which ought to be by destruction), or force, fear, fraud or even undue influence. The law in this area is not known for the speed at which it changes, although the Wills Act 1837 has now been overtaken by the Administration of Estates Act 1982. On this basis there will be another change along in 2127.

GENERAL GLOSSARY

Brief – Description which script writers believe criminals give their barristers; in fact, the set of papers prepared by the solicitor for the barrister to conduct the trial.

Brief fee – Exorbitant sum due to the barrister on delivery of the brief which should at least cover all preparation for the trial; sadly (for the client) non returnable even if the case then settles.

Refresher – Further large sum which reaches the parts (second and subsequent days of trial) that the brief fee cannot reach.

Door of court settlement – Near certain outcome of the case, enabling the barrister to leave for the golf course at 11.30 a.m. with the non-refundable brief fee safely secured.

Reasonable prospects of success – Conclusion of barrister's written opinion, meaning any fool can win this case but don't blame me if we lose.

Court List – Panic inducing list produced by the court at 4.00 p.m. announcing your case is now listed for the following morning at 10.00 a.m. (enabling you to notify 20 witnesses, cancel your appointments, and discover your barrister is 'double booked' in Newcastle Crown Court).

Discovery – Process of detailing in huge chronological list the ten cardboard boxes of random but crucial paperwork discovered by your client at unpredictable intervals (after he first told you that he has given you everything of relevance).

Pleadings – Lovingly crafted documents setting out the nature of the case, created at vast expense and then regularly amended once you work out what the other side is driving at.

Settling – Posh name for process of the barrister preparing pleadings.

Drafting – Posh name for the process of getting it wrong first time so you can charge for getting it right next time.

Automatic Directions – Draconian time limits imposed by the court so that slow solicitors can themselves be sued for negligence by their clients whose cases have been struck out.

Skeletons – Court requirement to make life easier for judges by setting out your hugely complex arguments for a ten day case on one side of A4 paper (should be kept in cupboards).

References – Reported judgments from earlier cases found in ancient books of law reports and wheeled to court in trolleys (so that the lawyers and the judges can each read a separate identical copy at the same time).

Reports – Not something you get free at the end of term, but the treatise your expert will run off his word processor if you pay his £500 fee.

Alibi warning – Read out by magistrates to give the defendant time to pretend he was somewhere else at the time.

Alibi – Guess by defendant as to where he might have been at the time (had he not been at the scene of the crime).

Sitting – What judges and magistrates do in court.

Bench – Equipment for above.

Retirement – Moment judge and magistrates decide to nip out for a coffee and a chat.

Adjournment – Longer moment to meet the other half for lunch.

All stand – Usher's announcement that judge has finally finished lunch.

Costs – Term for payment which to lawyers means a reasonable living and, to clients, a diabolical liberty.

Bill of costs – Statutory 78-page summary of every letter written and every task performed by lawyers which adds not inconsiderably to the cost of the bill.

Taxation of costs – Tortuous court process of forcing lawyers to catalogue every letter written and every task performed in order that each item can then be shot down in flames (usually at their expense).

Justice – What lawyers try to remember is more important than their clients or their costs.

THE AUTHOR

Martin Vernon's alias is a futile attempt to avoid these writings causing him to be struck off, or sent to a car-manufacturing city disconcertingly close to where he practises.

At the age of nine he was despatched to Sussex where he spent seven years dressed in knee breeches and yellow stockings marching up and down to a band. These peculiar traits, combined with the failure of his studies in Maths, Physics and Chemistry, inexorably led to a career in the law. He has pursued the sport of litigation in the Midlands, in London, occasionally in Europe, and now in hiding. He regards squash as the only proper alternative activity, perhaps influenced by his disabilities at tennis, golf, windsurfing, skiing and sex.

Observation of the failures of others during his time spent as a divorce lawyer has sustained his own happy marriage and amused his long-suffering family. A senior partner within his firm, he has been heard to observe that a partnership is like marriage, but that he never expected to have twenty-seven spouses, nor that only four of them would be women.

THE BLUFFER'S GUIDES™